Table of Contents

Patriotic Poke Cake 4

Wave Your Flag Cheesecake 6

Banana Split Pie 8

Melon Bubbles 10

Floating Fruit Parfaits 12

Strawberry-Orange Delight 14

Triple-Berry Cheesecake Tart 16

Chocolate Dream Pudding Pie 18

Frosty Orange Dream Squares 20

Sparkling Lemon Ice 22

Frozen Chocolate "Soufflés" 24

Frozen Lemonade Squares 26

Angel Lush with Pineapple 28

Easy Pudding Milk Shakes 30

Patriotic Poke Cake

PREP: 30 min. plus refrigerating • MAKES: 16 servings, 1 slice each.

WHAT YOU NEED

- 2 baked round white cake layers (9 inch), cooled
- 2 cups boiling water, divided
- 1 pkg. (4-serving size) **JELL-O** Strawberry Flavor Gelatin, or any other red flavor
- 1 pkg. (4-serving size) **JELL-O** Berry Blue Flavor Gelatin
- 1 tub (8 oz.) **COOL WHIP** Whipped Topping, thawed, divided

MAKE IT

PLACE cake layers, top-sides up, in 2 clean (9-inch) round cake pans. Pierce cakes with large fork at ½-inch intervals.

STIR 1 cup of the boiling water into each flavor dry gelatin mix in separate small bowls 2 min. until completely dissolved. Carefully pour red gelatin over 1 cake layer and blue gelatin over remaining cake layer. Refrigerate 3 hours.

DIP 1 cake pan in warm water 10 sec.; unmold onto serving plate. Spread with about 1 cup whipped topping. Unmold second cake layer; carefully place on first cake layer. Frost top and side of cake with remaining whipped topping. Refrigerate 1 hour or until ready to serve. Cut into 16 slices to serve. Store leftover cake in refrigerator.

Substitute: Prepare as directed, using **COOL WHIP LITE** Whipped Topping.

Patriotic Poke Cake with Cream Cheese Frosting: Pour gelatin over cake layers and refrigerate as directed. Unmold 1 of the layers onto serving plate; set aside. Beat 2 pkg. (8 oz. each) softened **PHILADELPHIA** Cream Cheese and 2 cups powdered sugar in large bowl with electric mixer on medium speed or wire whisk until well blended. Gently stir in whipped topping until well blended. Spread onto cake layer on plate as directed; top with second cake layer. Continue as directed.

Special Extra: Serve with colorful fresh berries, such as blueberries, strawberries and raspberries.

Wave Your Flag Cheesecake

PREP: 20 min. plus refrigerating • MAKES: 20 servings, 1 piece each.

WHAT YOU NEED

- 1 qt. strawberries, divided
- 1½ cups boiling water
- 1 pkg. (8-serving size) or 2 pkg. (4-serving size each) **JELL-O** Gelatin, any red flavor
- Ice cubes
- 1 cup cold water
- 1 pkg. (10.75 oz.) prepared pound cake, cut into 10 slices
- 1⅓ cups blueberries, divided
- 2 pkg. (8 oz. each) **PHILADELPHIA** Cream Cheese, softened
- ¼ cup sugar
- 1 tub (8 oz.) **COOL WHIP** Whipped Topping, thawed

MAKE IT

SLICE 1 cup of the strawberries. Halve remaining strawberries; set aside. Stir boiling water into dry gelatin mix in large bowl 2 min. or until completely dissolved. Add enough ice to cold water to measure 2 cups. Add to gelatin; stir until ice is melted. Refrigerate 5 min. or until slightly thickened (consistency of unbeaten egg whites).

MEANWHILE, cover bottom of 13×9-inch dish with cake. Stir sliced strawberries and 1 cup blueberries into gelatin. Spoon over cake. Refrigerate 4 hours or until set.

BEAT cream cheese and sugar in large bowl with wire whisk until well blended; gently stir in whipped topping. Spread over gelatin. Top with strawberry halves and remaining blueberries to resemble flag. Store in refrigerator.

> **Make Ahead:** Make dessert the day before. Top with fruit just before serving.

Banana Split Pie

PREP: 15 min. plus refrigerating • MAKES: 8 servings, 1 slice each.

WHAT YOU NEED

- 2 cups cold milk
- 2 pkg. (4-serving size each) **JELL-O** Vanilla Flavor Instant Pudding
- 1 graham cracker pie crust (6 oz.)
- 1 cup sliced strawberries, divided
- 1 banana, sliced
- 1 tub (8 oz.) **COOL WHIP** Whipped Topping, thawed, divided
- 2 Tbsp. chocolate syrup

MAKE IT

POUR milk into large bowl. Add dry pudding mixes. Beat with wire whisk 2 min. Spread 1½ cups of the pudding onto bottom of crust.

TOP with half of the strawberries; cover with bananas. Add half of the whipped topping to remaining pudding; stir gently until well blended. Spread over fruit layer in crust. Spread remaining whipped topping over pie to within 1 inch of crust. Drizzle with chocolate syrup; top with remaining strawberries.

REFRIGERATE 3 hours or until set. Store leftovers in refrigerator.

Healthy Living: Save 100 calories and 5 grams of fat per serving by preparing with fat-free milk, **JELL-O** Vanilla Flavor Fat Free Sugar Free Instant Pudding, a ready-to-use reduced-fat graham cracker crumb crust and **COOL WHIP LITE** Whipped Topping.

Special Extra: Garnish with ¼ cup **PLANTERS** Pecan Pieces just before serving.

Melon Bubbles

PREP: 15 min. plus refrigerating • MAKES: 8 servings.

WHAT YOU NEED

- 1½ cups boiling water
- 2 pkg. (4-serving size each) **JELL-O** Melon Fusion Flavor Gelatin
- 2½ cups cold club soda
- ⅓ cup each: cantaloupe, honeydew and watermelon balls

MAKE IT

STIR boiling water into dry gelatin mixes in large bowl at least 2 min. until completely dissolved. Stir in club soda. Refrigerate 1½ hours or until thickened (spoon drawn through leaves definite impression).

MEASURE 1 cup thickened gelatin into medium bowl; set aside. Stir melon balls into remaining gelatin. Spoon into 8 dessert glasses.

BEAT reserved gelatin with electric mixer on high speed until fluffy and about doubled in volume. Spoon over gelatin in glasses. Refrigerate 3 hours or until firm. Store leftovers in refrigerator.

> **Substitute:** Substitute seltzer for the club soda.

> **Substitute:** Prepare as directed, using 1 pkg. (8-serving size) or 2 pkg. (4-serving size each) **JELL-O** Lemon Flavor Sugar Free Gelatin.

Floating Fruit Parfaits

PREP: 15 min. plus refrigerating • MAKES: 6 servings.

WHAT YOU NEED

- ½ cup sliced strawberries
- ¾ cup boiling water
- 1 pkg. (0.3 oz.) **JELL-O** Strawberry Flavor Sugar Free Gelatin
- ½ cup cold water
- ¾ cup ice cubes
- 1 cup plus 6 Tbsp. thawed **COOL WHIP LITE** Whipped Topping, divided

MAKE IT

SPOON berries into 6 parfait or dessert glasses. Add boiling water to dry gelatin mix in medium bowl; stir 2 min. until completely dissolved. Add cold water and ice cubes; stir until ice is melted. Pour ¾ cup gelatin over berries. Refrigerate 20 min. or until gelatin is set but not firm.

ADD 1 cup whipped topping to remaining gelatin; whisk until well blended. Spoon over gelatin in glasses.

REFRIGERATE 1 hour or until firm. Serve topped with the remaining whipped topping.

> **Variation:** Prepare as directed, using **JELL-O** Orange Flavor Sugar Free Gelatin and substituting cantaloupe balls for the strawberries.

> **Storing Fresh Fruit:** Most fruits keep best when stored in the refrigerator. Berries, cherries and plums should not be washed before refrigeration, since excess moisture will cause these fruits to spoil more quickly.

> **Nutrition Bonus:** Satisfy your sweet tooth with this elegant low-fat dessert. As a bonus, the strawberries provide a good source of vitamin C.

Special Extra: Add ½ cup seedless grapes with the strawberries.

Strawberry-Orange Delight

PREP: 15 min. plus refrigerating • **MAKES:** 16 servings, about ½ cup each.

WHAT YOU NEED

- 2½ cups boiling water
- 3 pkg. (4-serving size each) **JELL-O** Strawberry Flavor Gelatin
- 2¾ cups cold water
- 1 can (11 oz.) mandarin orange segments, drained
- 4 oz. (½ of 8-oz. pkg.) **PHILADELPHIA** Cream Cheese, softened
- 2 Tbsp. sugar
- 1 tub (8 oz.) **COOL WHIP** Whipped Topping, thawed, divided

MAKE IT

STIR boiling water into dry gelatin mixes in medium bowl at least 2 min. until completely dissolved. Stir in cold water. Refrigerate about 1¼ hours or until slightly thickened (consistency of unbeaten egg whites). Reserve a few oranges for garnish. Gently stir remaining oranges into thickened gelatin. Set aside.

BEAT cream cheese and sugar in separate medium bowl with wire whisk until well blended. Gently stir in 2 cups whipped topping. Spoon into large serving bowl; cover with the gelatin mixture.

REFRIGERATE 2 hours or until firm. Top with remaining whipped topping and reserved oranges just before serving.

> **How to Soften Cream Cheese:** Place measured amount of cream cheese in microwaveable bowl. Microwave on HIGH 10 sec. or until slightly softened.

Triple-Berry Cheesecake Tart

PREP: 15 min. plus refrigerating • **MAKES:** 10 servings.

WHAT YOU NEED

- 1¼ cups finely crushed vanilla wafers (about 45 wafers)
- ¼ cup (½ stick) butter, melted
- 1 pkg. (8 oz.) PHILADELPHIA Cream Cheese, softened
- ¼ cup sugar
- 1 cup thawed COOL WHIP Whipped Topping
- 2 cups mixed berries (raspberries, sliced strawberries, blueberries)
- ¾ cup boiling water
- 1 pkg. (4-serving size) JELL-O Lemon Flavor Gelatin
- 1 cup ice cubes

MAKE IT

MIX wafer crumbs and butter; press firmly onto bottom and up side of 9-inch tart pan. Place in freezer while preparing filling.

BEAT cream cheese and sugar in large bowl with electric mixer on medium speed until well blended. Gently stir in whipped topping. Spoon into crust. Top with berries. Cover and refrigerate while preparing gelatin.

STIR boiling water into dry gelatin mix in medium bowl 2 min. until completely dissolved. Add ice cubes; stir until ice is completely melted. Refrigerate 15 min., or until slightly thickened (consistency of unbeaten egg whites). Spoon gelatin over fruit in pan. Refrigerate 3 hours or until set. Store leftover tart in refrigerator.

> **Size-Wise:** This colorful berry dessert makes a great treat to share with friends and family.

Chocolate Dream Pudding Pie

PREP: *15 min. plus freezing* • **MAKES:** *8 servings, 1 slice each.*

WHAT YOU NEED

- 1 cup cold milk
- 1 pkg. (4-serving size) **JELL-O** Chocolate Instant Pudding
- 2½ cups thawed **COOL WHIP** Whipped Topping, divided
- 1 chocolate cookie pie crust (6 oz.)
- 2 Tbsp. hot fudge ice cream topping

MAKE IT

POUR milk into large bowl. Add dry pudding mix. Beat with wire whisk 2 min. or until well blended. Gently stir in 1½ cups whipped topping. Spoon into crust. Cover with remaining whipped topping.

FREEZE 6 hours or until firm.

REMOVE pie from freezer about 15 min. before serving. Let stand at room temperature to soften slightly. Meanwhile, heat hot fudge topping as directed on label; drizzle over pie. Store leftovers in freezer.

> **Size-Wise:** A slice of this pie goes a long way on chocolate flavor.

Frosty Orange Dream Squares

PREP: 15 min. plus freezing • MAKES: 9 servings.

WHAT YOU NEED

- 40 vanilla wafers, finely crushed (about 1½ cups)
- ¼ cup (½ stick) butter, melted
- 2 pkg. (3.4 oz. each) **JELL-O** Vanilla Flavor Instant Pudding (see Note below)
- 2 cups cold milk
- 1 tub (8 oz.) **COOL WHIP** Whipped Topping, thawed, divided
- 2 cups orange sherbet, softened

MAKE IT

LINE 13×9-inch pan with foil, with ends of foil extending over sides. Mix wafer crumbs and butter. Press onto bottom of prepared pan; set aside.

BEAT dry pudding mixes and milk in medium bowl with whisk 2 min. Stir in ½ of the whipped topping. Spoon over crust. Refrigerate 10 min. Add remaining whipped topping to sherbet; whisk until well blended. Spoon over pudding layer; cover.

FREEZE 3 hours. Use foil handles to remove dessert from pan before cutting to serve.

> **Note from the Kraft Kitchens:** For best texture, do not prepare recipe with **JELL-O** Fat Free Sugar Free Instant Pudding.

Sparkling Lemon Ice

PREP: *20 min. plus freezing* • **MAKES:** *6 servings.*

WHAT YOU NEED

- 1 cup boiling water
- 1 pkg. (4-serving size) **JELL-O** Lemon Flavor Sugar Free Gelatin
- 1 cup cold lemon lime-flavored seltzer
- ½ tsp. grated lemon zest
- 3 Tbsp. fresh lemon juice

MAKE IT

STIR boiling water into dry gelatin mix in medium bowl at least 2 min. until completely dissolved. Stir in remaining ingredients. Pour into 9-inch square pan; cover.

FREEZE 3 hours or until frozen.

REMOVE from freezer; let stand at room temperature 10 min. to soften slightly. Beat with electric mixer on high speed until smooth. Spoon into 6 martini glasses or dessert dishes to serve. Store leftovers in freezer.

> **Use Your Blender:** Use an electric blender to beat the partially frozen gelatin mixture instead of the electric mixer.

> **Nutrition Bonus:** Cool off with this low-calorie, fat-free lemon ice.

Special Extra: Garnish with fresh lemon slices and mint sprigs.

Frozen Chocolate "Soufflés"

PREP: 10 min. plus freezing • **MAKES:** 8 servings, 1 "soufflé" each.

WHAT YOU NEED

- 3 cups milk
- 1 pkg. (8-serving size) or 2 pkg. (4-serving size each) **JELL-O** Chocolate Instant Pudding
- 2 cups thawed **COOL WHIP** Whipped Topping
- 16 chocolate sandwich cookies, finely chopped (about 2 cups)
- 8 maraschino cherries

MAKE IT

POUR milk into medium bowl. Add dry pudding mix. Beat with wire whisk 2 min. Gently stir in whipped topping.

SPOON 2 Tbsp. of the chopped cookies into each of 8 (8- to 9-oz.) paper drinking cups. Cover evenly with half of the pudding mixture. Press gently with the back of a spoon to eliminate air pockets. Repeat layers. Cover with foil.

FREEZE 5 hours or until firm. Remove from freezer about 15 min. before serving. Let stand at room temperature to soften slightly. Peel away paper to unmold onto dessert plates. Top each with a cherry. Store leftovers in freezer.

Variation: Prepare as directed, using **JELL-O** Vanilla Flavor Instant Pudding and chocolate chip cookies.

Frozen Lemonade Squares

PREP: 20 min. plus freezing • MAKES: 9 servings.

WHAT YOU NEED

- 9 graham crackers, finely crushed (about 1¼ cups)
- ⅓ cup margarine or butter, melted
- 1 qt. (4 cups) frozen vanilla yogurt, softened
- 6 oz. (½ of 12-oz. can) frozen lemonade concentrate, thawed
- ½ cup thawed **COOL WHIP LITE** Whipped Topping

MAKE IT

MIX graham crumbs and margarine; press onto bottom of 9-inch square pan.

BEAT yogurt and concentrate with mixer until well blended; spread over crust.

FREEZE 4 hours or until firm. Serve topped with whipped topping.

> **Note:** Empty the remaining lemonade concentrate into small pitcher. Stir in 1½ cans water. Refrigerate until ready to serve over ice in tall glasses.

> **Size-Wise:** Looking for a special treat? Try a serving of this frosty lemon dessert.

Special Extra: Garnish with fresh mint sprigs and lemon slices.

Angel Lush with Pineapple

PREP: 15 min. plus refrigerating • MAKES: 10 servings.

WHAT YOU NEED

- 1 can (20 oz.) crushed pineapple in juice, undrained
- 1 pkg. (3.4 oz.) **JELL-O** Vanilla Flavor Instant Pudding
- 1 cup thawed **COOL WHIP** Whipped Topping
- 1 pkg. (10 oz.) round angel food cake, cut into 3 layers
- 1 cup mixed berries

MAKE IT

MIX pineapple and dry pudding mix. Gently stir in whipped topping.

STACK cake layers on plate, spreading pudding mixture between layers and on top of cake.

REFRIGERATE 1 hour. Top with berries.

Variation: Prepare using 1 pkg. (1 oz.) **JELL-O** Vanilla Flavor Fat Free Sugar Free Instant Pudding and **COOL WHIP LITE** Whipped Topping.

How to Cut Cake: Use toothpicks to mark cake into 3 layers. Use a serrated knife to cut cake, in sawing motion, into layers.

Lemon-Berry Lush with Pineapple: Prepare using **JELL-O** Lemon Flavor Instant Pudding.

Easy Pudding Milk Shakes

PREP: 5 min. • *MAKES:* 5 servings, 1¼ cups each.

WHAT YOU NEED

- 3 cups cold fat-free milk
- 1 pkg. (4-serving size) **JELL-O** Chocolate Fat Free Sugar Free Instant Pudding
- 3 scoops (about 1½ cups) fat-free no-sugar-added vanilla ice cream

MAKE IT

POUR milk into blender. Add dry pudding mix and ice cream; blend on high speed 15 sec. or until well blended.

SERVE immediately. (Or, refrigerate until ready to serve, stirring just before serving. Mixture thickens as it stands. Thin with additional milk, if desired.)

Variation: Prepare as directed, using 2% or whole milk, regular **JELL-O** Instant Pudding and your favorite flavor of regular ice cream.

Substitute: Prepare as directed, using **JELL-O** Vanilla Flavor Fat Free Sugar Free Instant Pudding.

Nutrition Bonus: An updated version of an old-time favorite, this creamy milk shake is low fat, saturated fat free and an excellent source of calcium.